INSPIRATIONAL

Coloring Book for Teenage Boys

With Motivational Quotes

Thank you for choosing this coloring book.

*If you like this book I'd really appreciate it if you'd leave me a review
and have a look at my other books.*

INSPIRATIONAL
Coloring Book for Teenage Boys

With Motivational Quotes

ISBN: 978-1-914997-15-0

Pocket Learner Publishing

Thank you for choosing this coloring book

If you like this book I'd really appreciate it if you'd leave me a review and have a look at my other books.

REFLECTIONS
Inspirational Coloring Journal for Women

REFLECTIONS
Inspirational Coloring Journal for Teenage Boys

REFLECTIONS
Inspirational Coloring Journal for Men

REFLECTIONS
Inspirational Coloring Journal for Adults

A range of guided and gratitude journals

A range of Activity Books

A selection of Log Books

Inspirational Coloring Book for Teenage Girls

Inspirational Coloring Book for Teenage Boys

Inspirational Coloring Book for Women

Inspirational Coloring Book for Men

Inspirational Coloring Book for Adults

Inspirational Coloring Book for Boys

Inspirational Coloring Book for Girls

Coloring book for kids aged 2-4, 4-8

A Gift for You

Please join our mailing list to receive periodic updates and materials. You'll also be able to keep abreast of our future publications.

As a thank you please visit the following page or scan the QR code to download a set of original inspirational posters that you can print out, frame and position in your favorite space.

http://eepurl.com/h8SU31

This coloring book belongs to:

_____

Cows don't coo, and
doves don't moo;
in all you are,
say and do,
be real, and true to you.

Don't be surprised
if your bird doesn't fly
if you keep it locked
in a cage.

Eagles have
no business in
chicken squabbles.

If you can't do it alone,
do it together;
and if you can't go
together, go it alone.

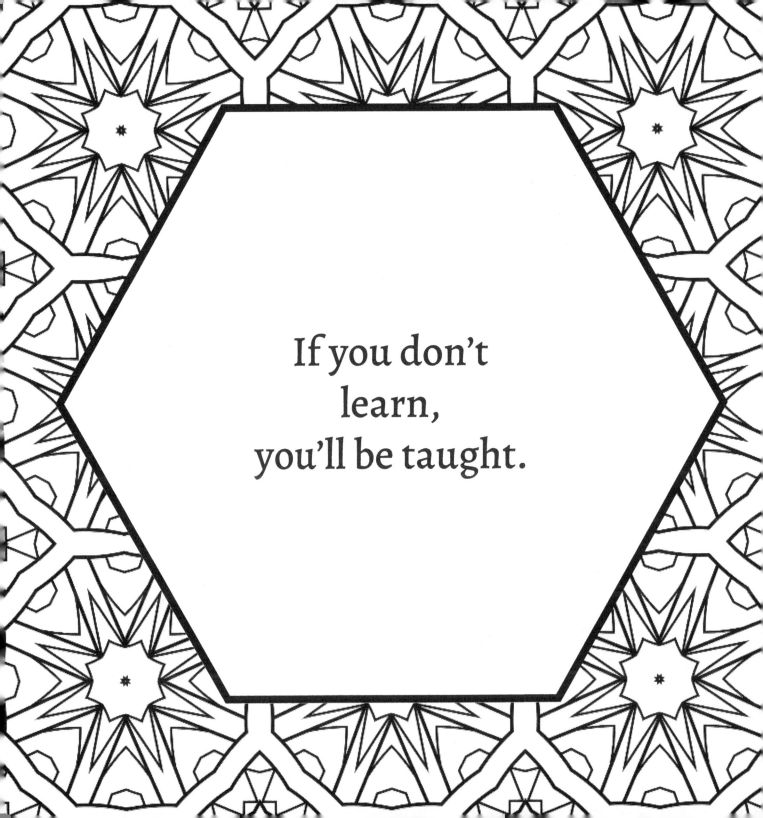

If you don't
learn,
you'll be taught.

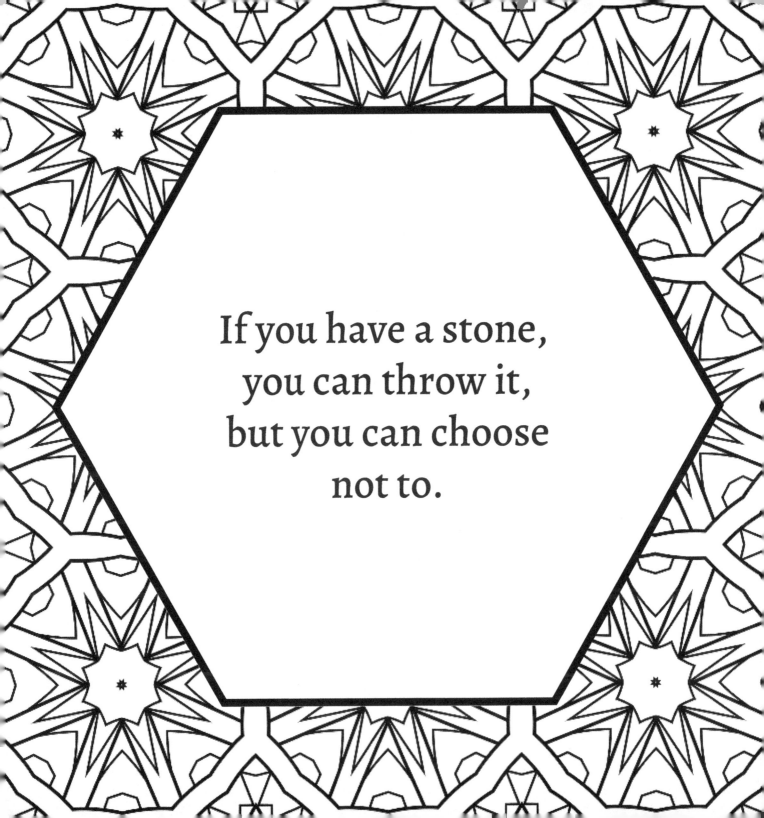

If you have a stone,
you can throw it,
but you can choose
not to.

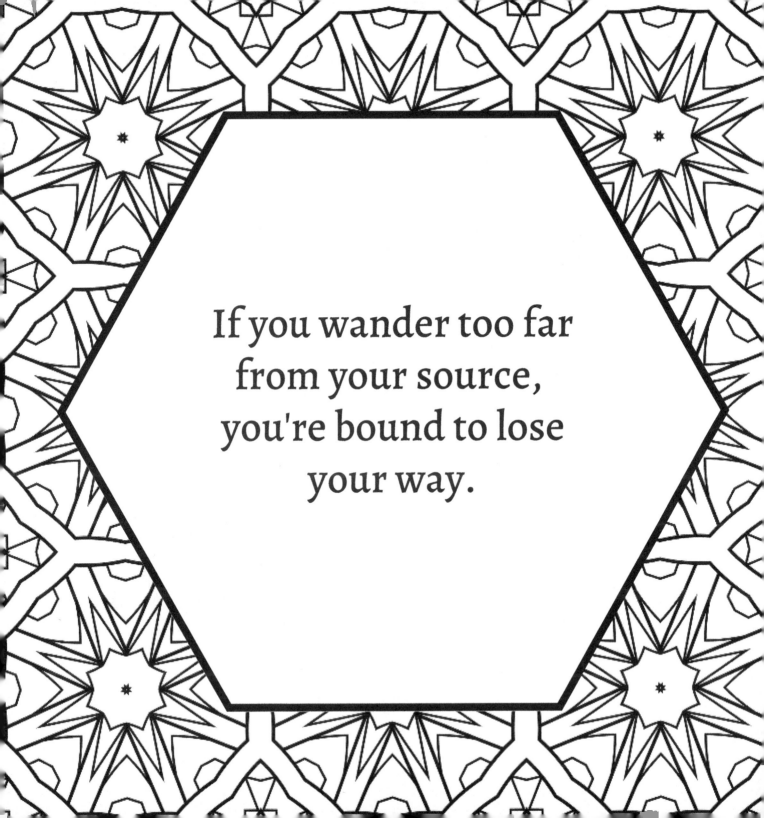

If you wander too far
from your source,
you're bound to lose
your way.

If you work your
gift,
your gift will work
for you.

If you're a go-getter,
you've got to go get
it!

If you're not prepared to serve, you're not equipped to lead; leadership is service.

If you're always
comfortable
and everything is easy,
you're not growing.

Ignorance isn't bliss
when your hair is
on fire.

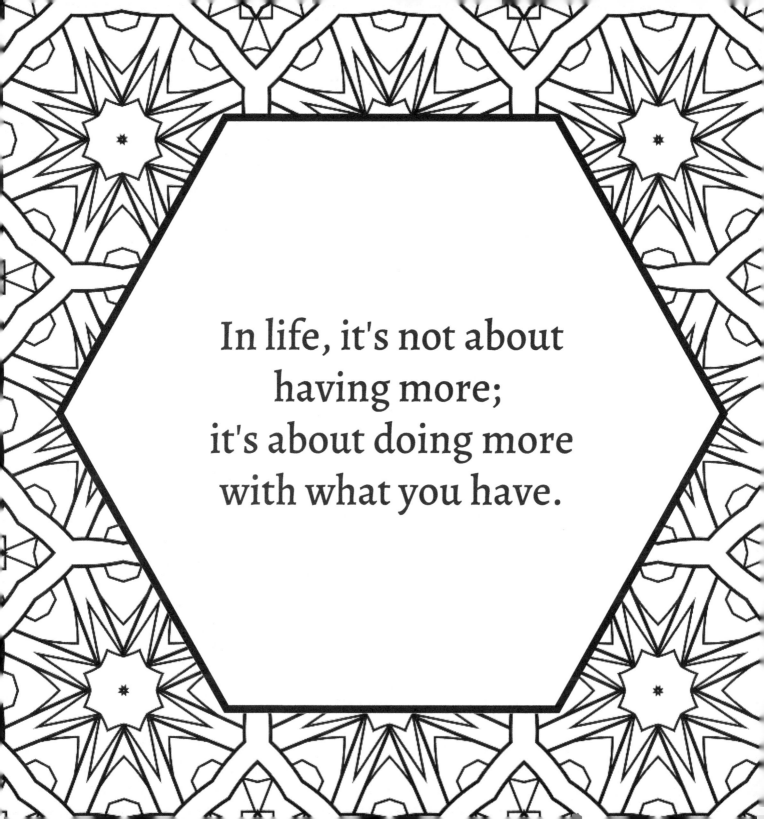

In life, it's not about
having more;
it's about doing more
with what you have.

In order to move
forward,
sometimes you've
got to stand still.

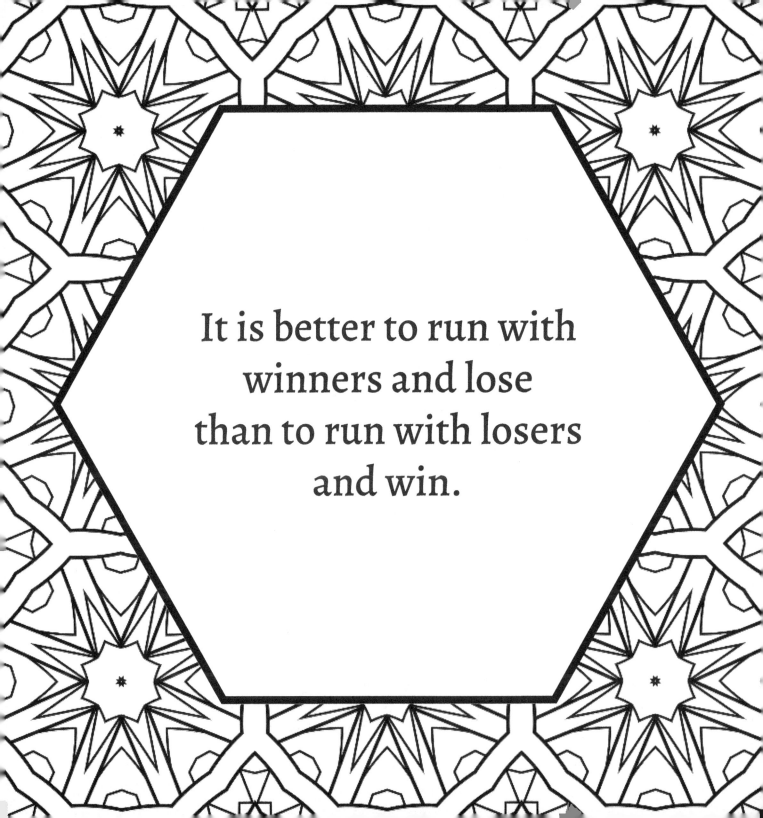

It is better to run with
winners and lose
than to run with losers
and win.

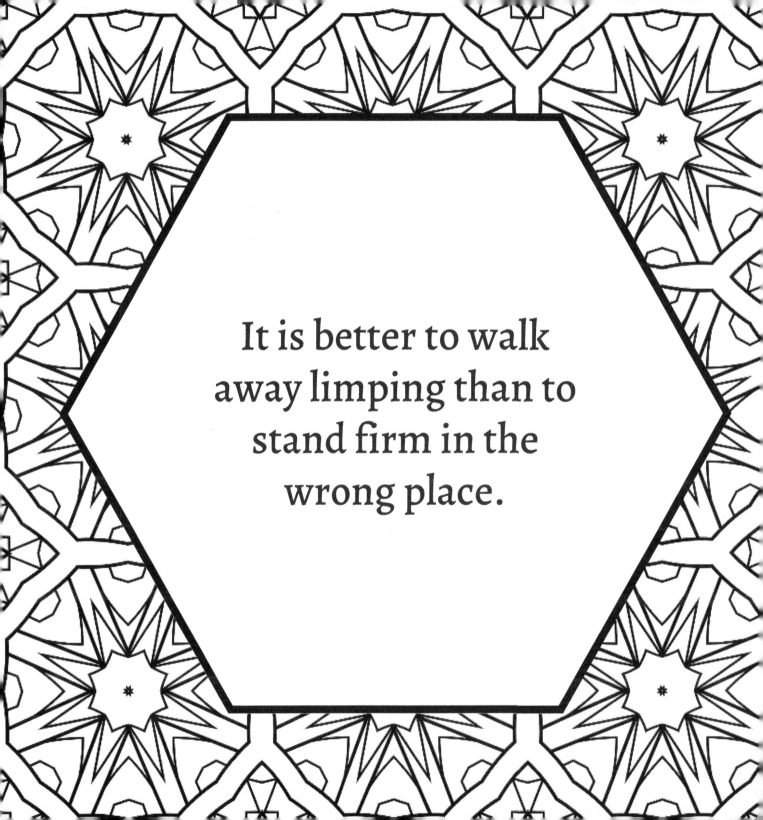

It is better to walk away limping than to stand firm in the wrong place.

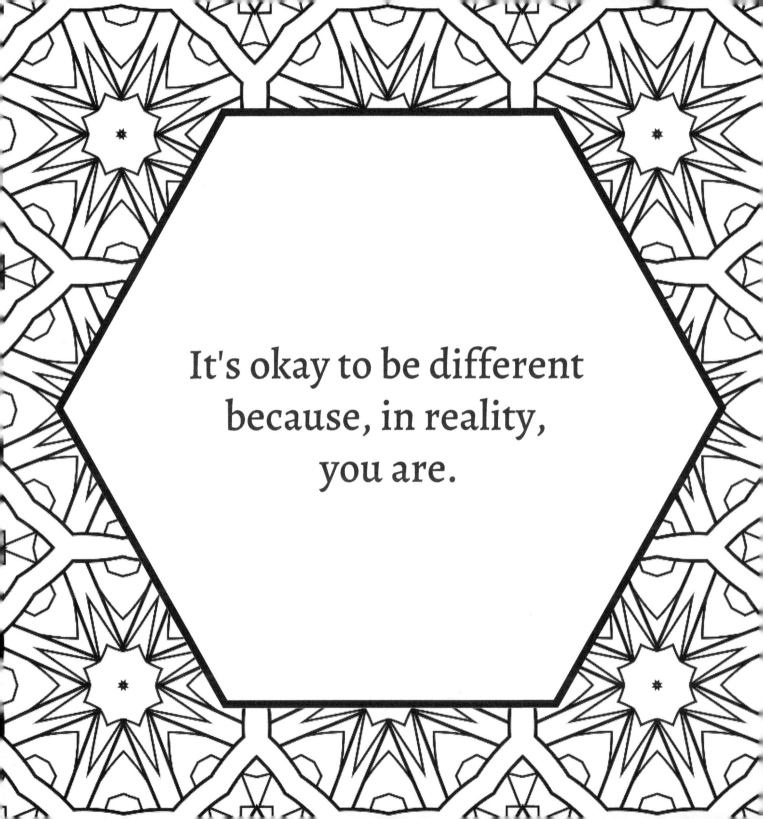

It's okay to be different because, in reality, you are.

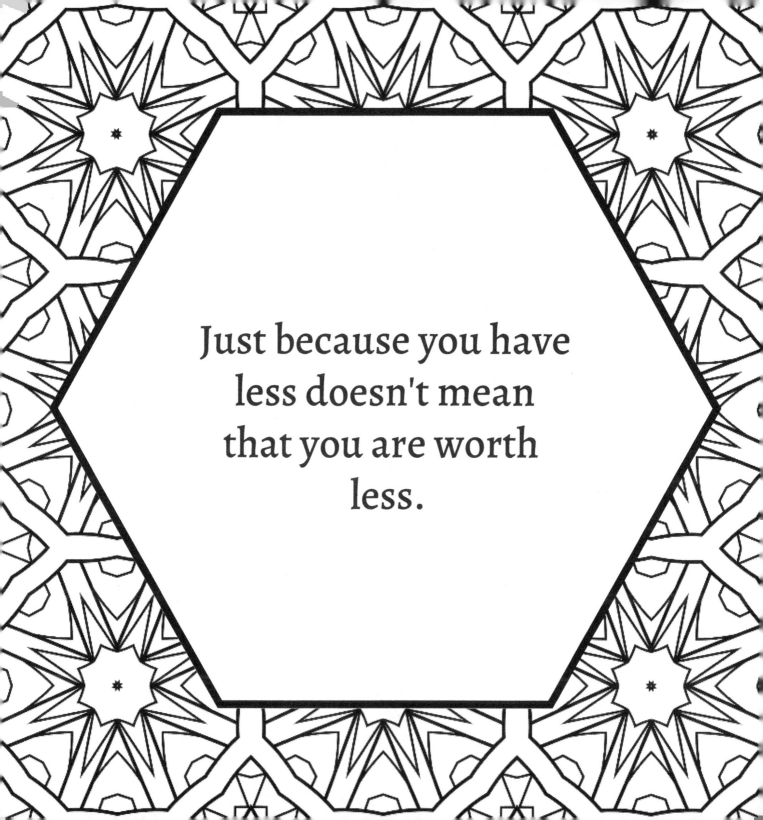

Just because you have less doesn't mean that you are worth less.

Just because your hand can reach it doesn't mean that you must pick it.

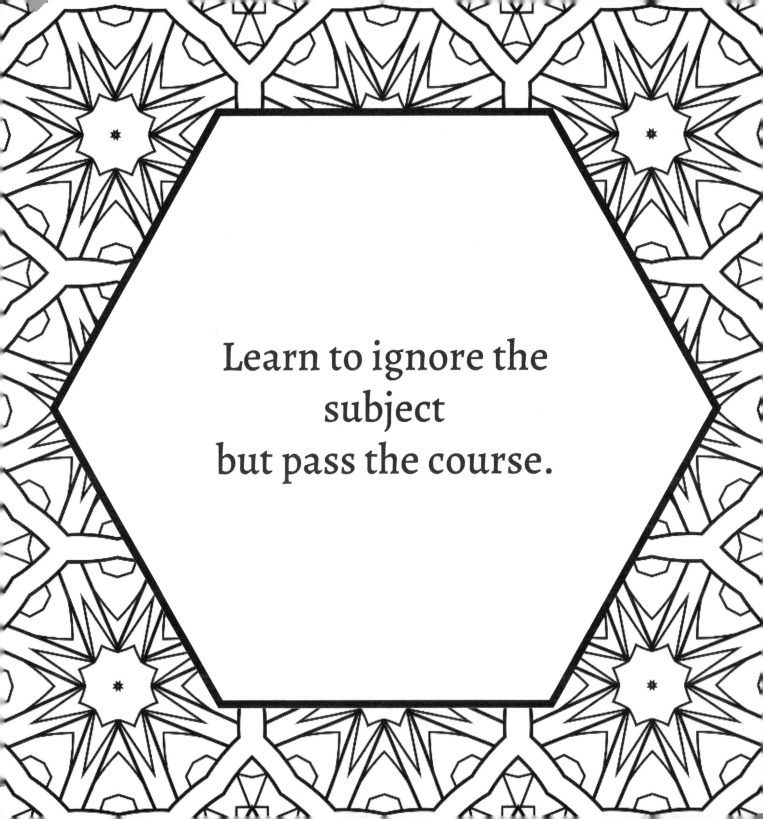

Learn to ignore the
subject
but pass the course.

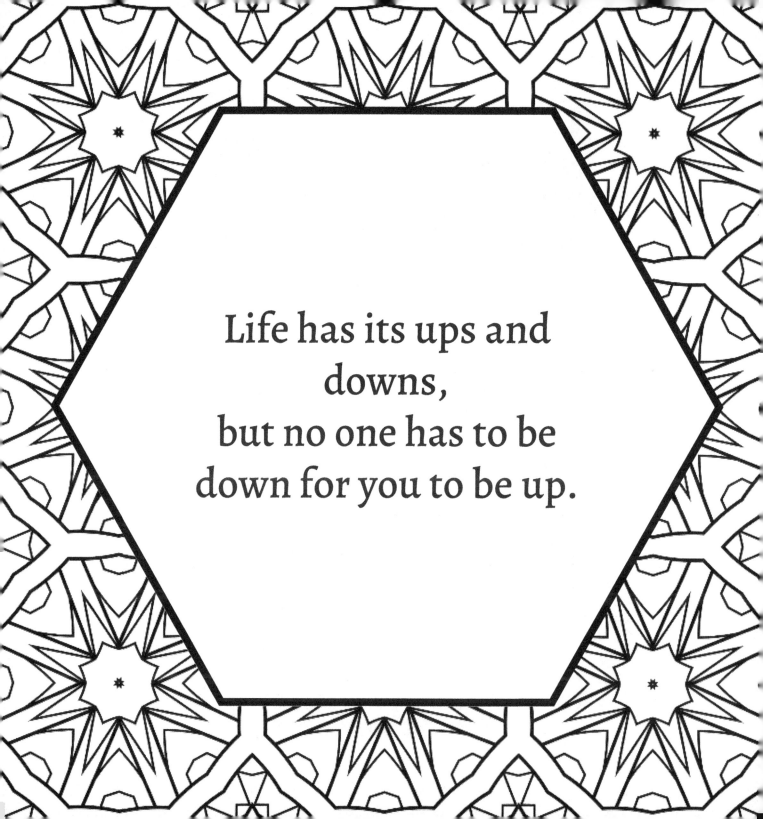

Life has its ups and
downs,
but no one has to be
down for you to be up.

Motivation gets you going,
passion keeps you going
but it's persistence that
gets you there.

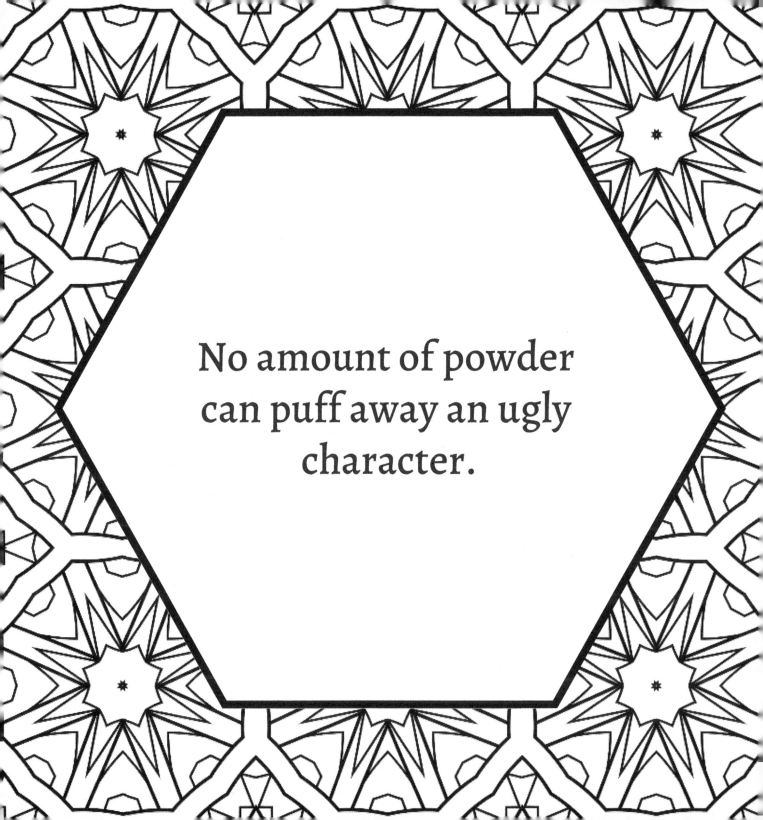

No amount of powder can puff away an ugly character.

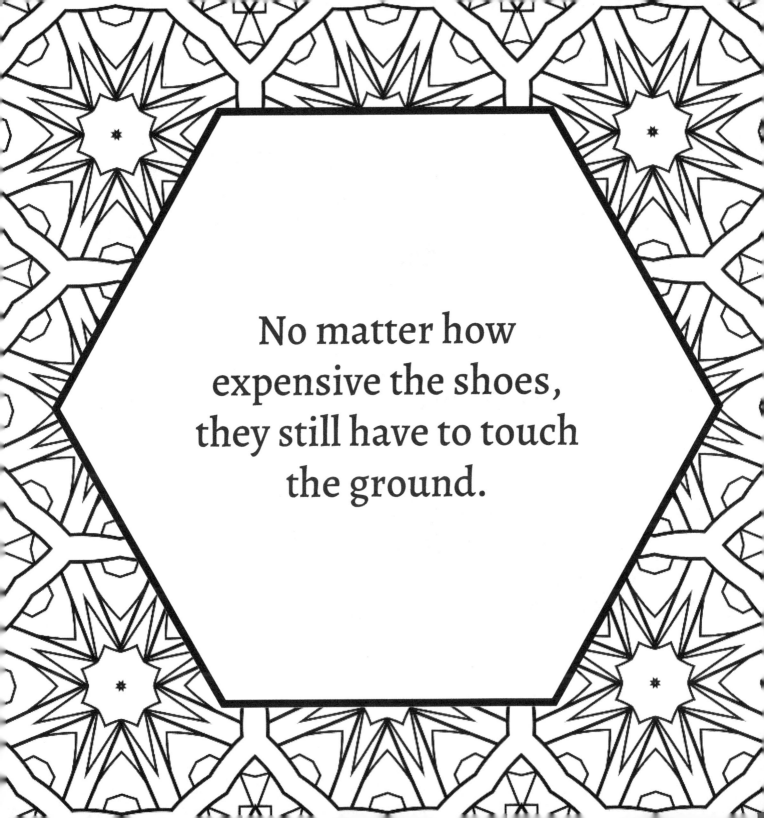

No matter how
expensive the shoes,
they still have to touch
the ground.

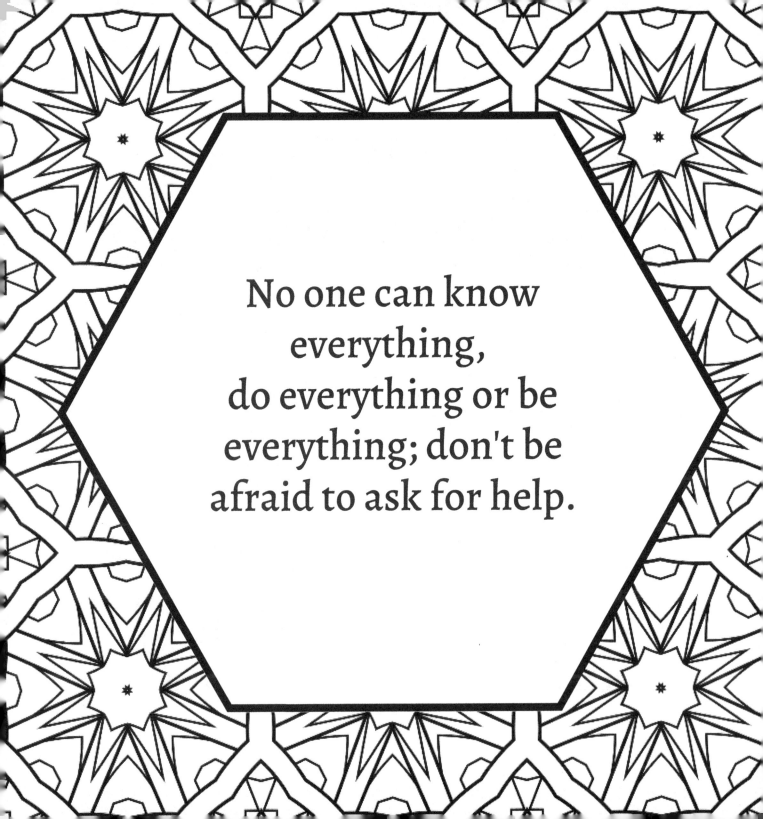

No one can know
everything,
do everything or be
everything; don't be
afraid to ask for help.

No one person can
do every single thing,
but every single
person can do one
thing.

Opportunities do
not appear
for those who don't
prepare.

Plan your journey
even if you don't
have a ride.

Sometimes it's
harder
to do nothing.

Sometimes the best
way to speak to
someone
is to say nothing.

Sow where you don't expect to reap.

Stepping stones
may look like
stumbling blocks.

Talent without
ambition
makes for wasted
gifting.

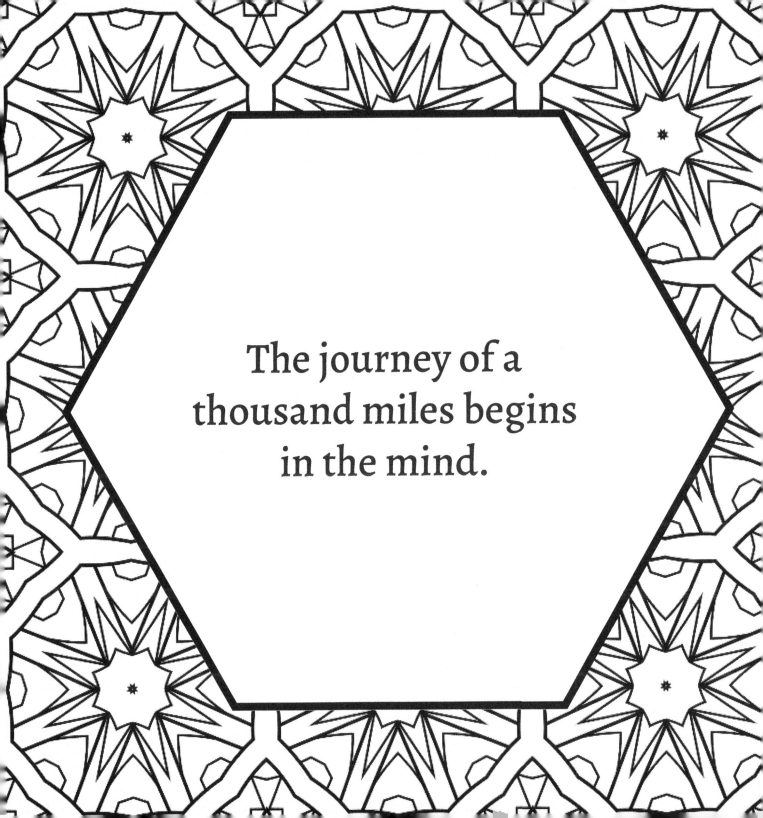

The journey of a
thousand miles begins
in the mind.

The pain is greater
when it's later.

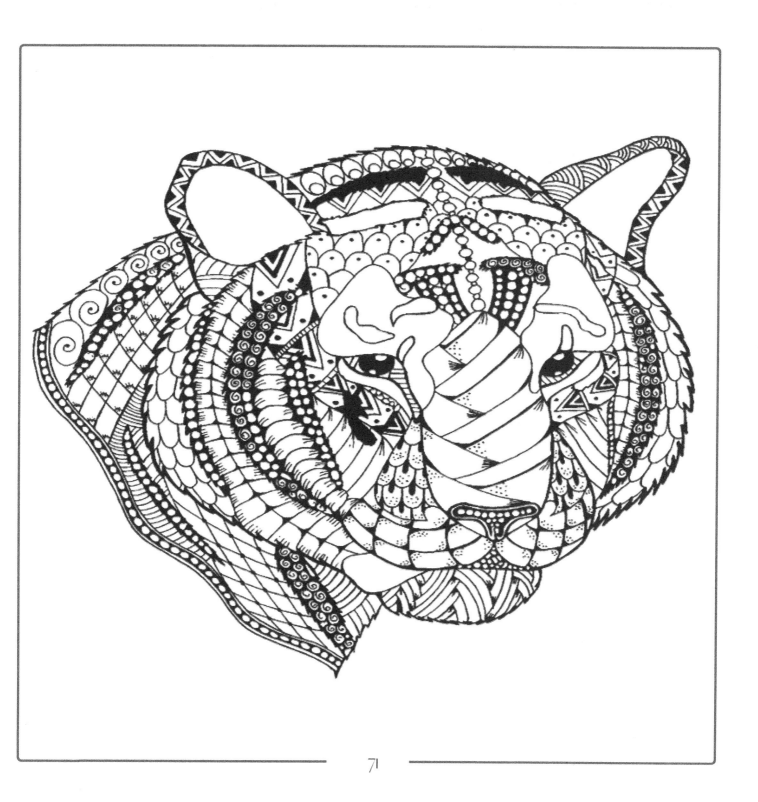

Those who have never failed have never tried.

Truth does not set
free where ignorance
is king.

Until you are willing
to take the first step,
don't think about the
next level.

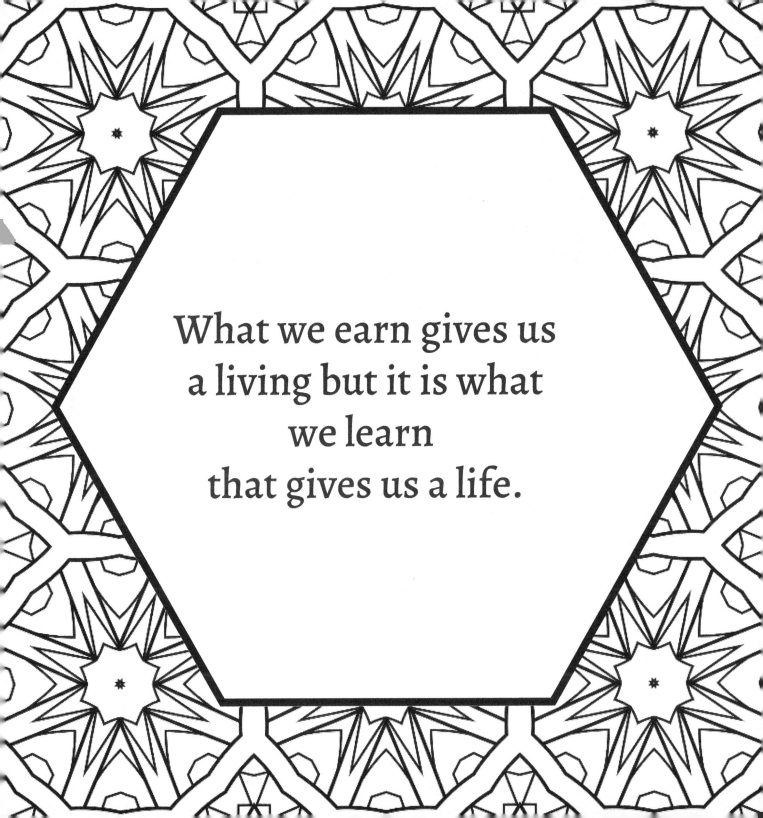

What we earn gives us
a living but it is what
we learn
that gives us a life.

When the ball falls
into the gutter,
it's time to get out
of the game.

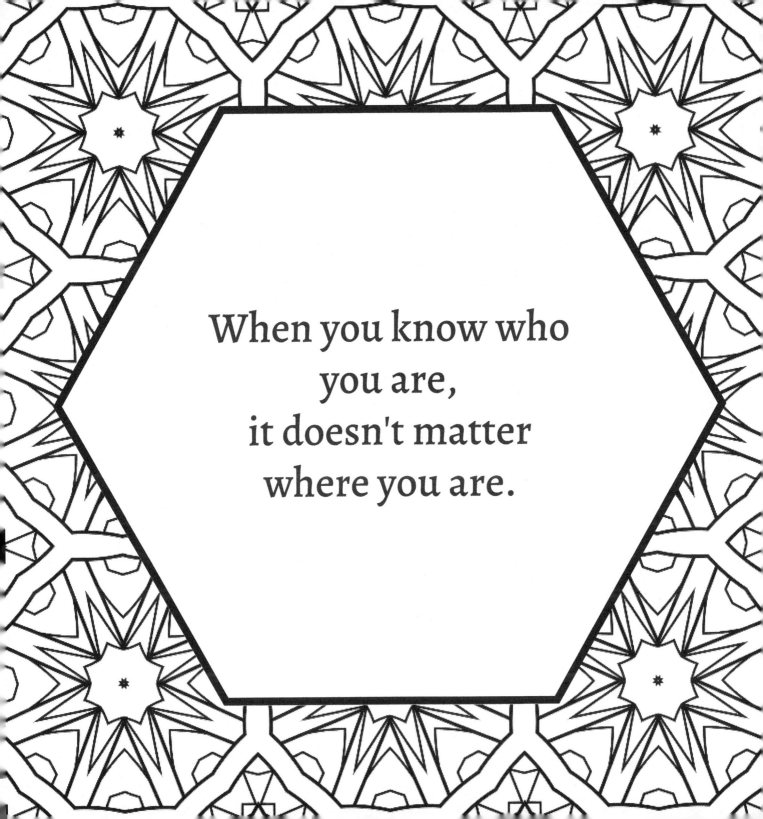

When you know who
you are,
it doesn't matter
where you are.

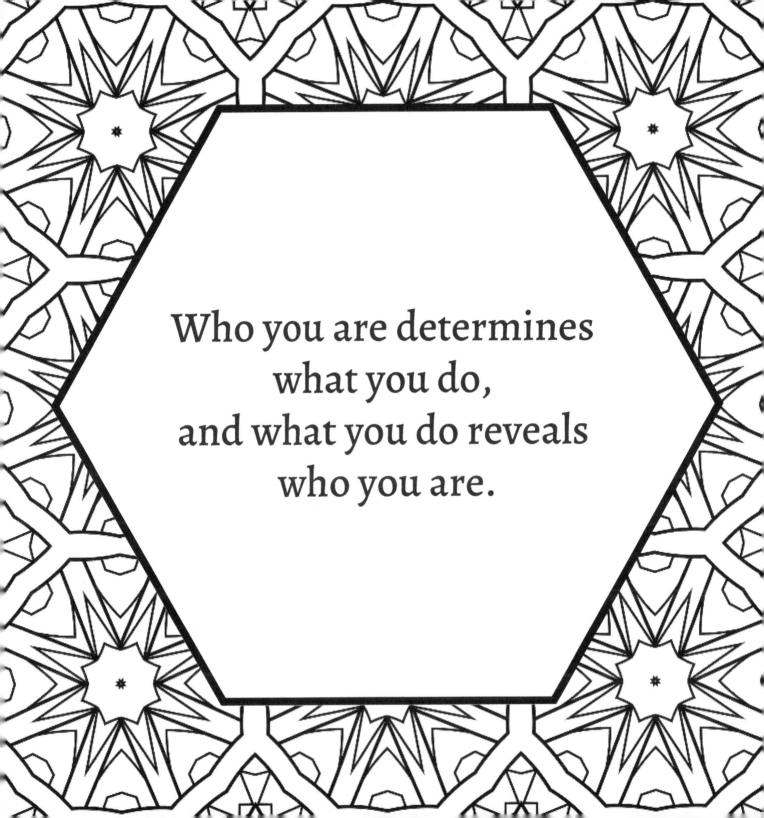

Who you are determines
what you do,
and what you do reveals
who you are.

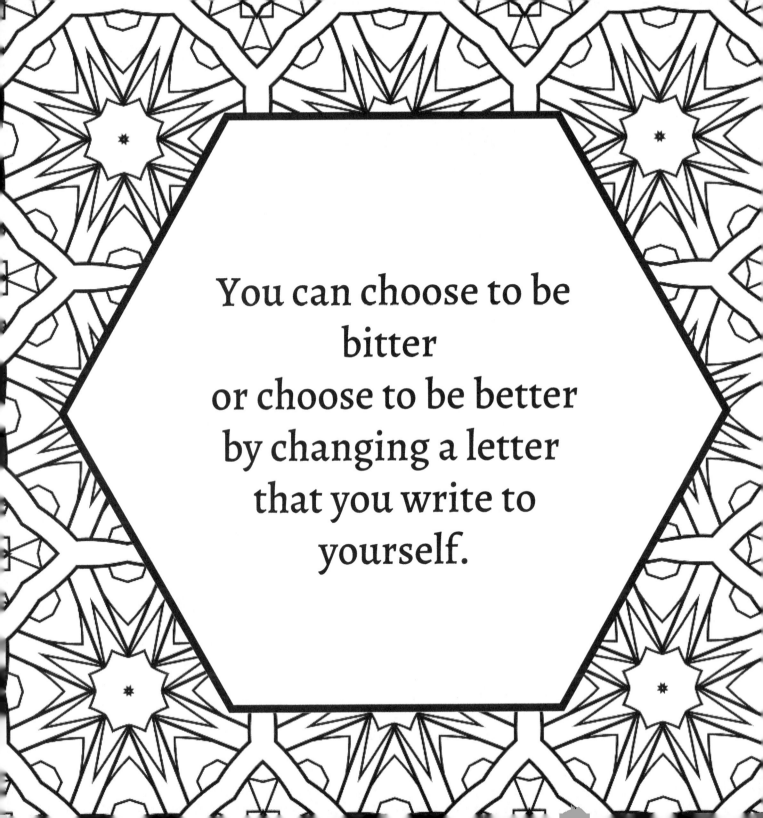

You can choose to be
bitter
or choose to be better
by changing a letter
that you write to
yourself.

You can do a good thing but it may not be the right thing.

You can't go places
with people who aren't
going anywhere.

You can't lock yourself
behind a door
and then complain that
no one is reaching out
to you.

You can't sit on it and expect it to move.

Your dream is planted
inside you;
don't worry if others can't
see it or don't share it.
Just don't let them
stifle it.

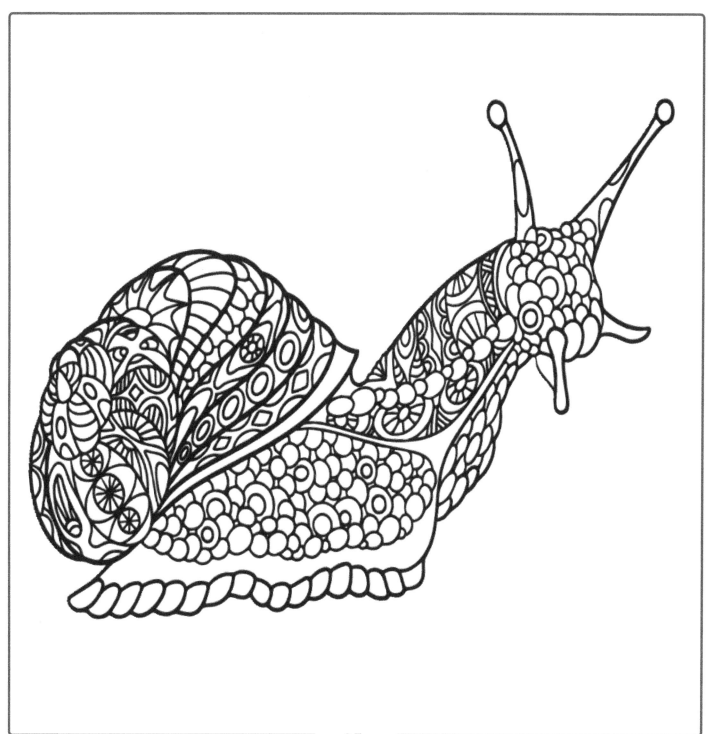

Your mentor is not
the person who
advises you;
it's the person
whose advice you
follow.

You can't curse
Caesar
in his Palace.

Made in the USA
Middletown, DE
07 June 2023